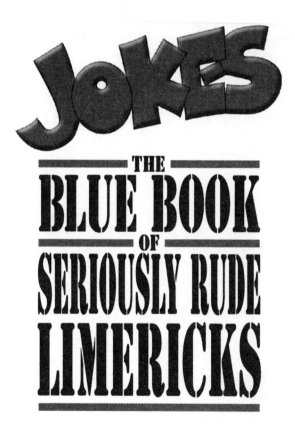

JOKES

THE
BLUE BOOK
OF
SERIOUSLY RUDE
LIMERICKS

MICHAEL HORGAN

Strathearn Publishing

Strathearn Publishing

PO Box 44, Slough, Berkshire, SL1 4YN
Trade Distribution by W. Foulsham & Co. Ltd
The Publishing House, Bennetts Close, Cippenham, Slough,
Berkshire, SL1 5AP, England

ISBN 0-572-02915-2

Printed in Great Britain by Cox & Wyman Ltd, Reading,
Berkshire

I thought she'd be naughty
    but nice,
And she proved to be cheap
    at the price,
    With big hairy legs
    And teats like fried eggs
And a twat that was
    tight as a vice.

When he woke with a
    pain in his head
And found someone else
    in his bed
with her legs open wide,
It wasn't his bride,
But her toothless old
    mother instead.

When a girl on an island
remote
Met a Frenchman who
lived in a boat,
She was soon in his bunk
With a mouth full of
spunk
And a ruddy great Frog
in her throat.

I know that you're probably right

That Nelly is not very bright,

But when we start screwing

She knows what she's

doing

And we screw

several times

every night.

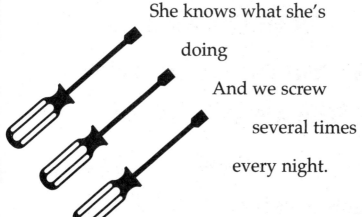

Fitzpatrick, Fitzgerald

and me

Are terribly gay company:

FitzP fits FitzG

And FitzG fits FitzP,

And each of those Fitzes

fits me!

A CLEVER YOUNG LADY
CALLED LU

FOUND A CHIMNEY SWEEP
STUCK UP THE FLUE,

SO SEIZING HER CHANCE

SHE PULLED DOWN HIS PANTS

AND RELIEVED WHAT HAD
CAUSED HIS TO-DO.

Though pandas do not
like to screw

And a panda's orgasms
are few,

The vet makes them come

Using fingers and thumb

And sprays the whole zoo
with their goo.

My new secretary,
Miss Pymme,
Seems frightfully proper
and prim,
And only I know
How she lets herself go
If you stuff twenty quid
up her quim.

TO MAKE FATHER'S CHRISTMAS EVE CHEERIER

OUR REVEREND MOTHER SUPERIOR

WEARS TRANSPARENT SCANTIES

AND OPEN-CROTCH PANTIES

AND TINSEL AROUND HER POSTERIOR.

HOW SAD TO SEE SOMEONE

LIKE YATES

IN SUCH IMPECUNIOUS STRAITS:

THE REASON, OF COURSE, IS

 FAST WOMEN,

SLOW HORSES

AND THE SAILORS HE FREQUENTLY

DATES.

THE REVEREND
VICAR OF BUDE

WHEN SLEEP-WALKING
TOTALLY NUDE,

ARRIVED QUITE BY
CHANCE

AT A CHARITY DANCE

AND TOSSED OFF
ALL OVER THE FOOD.

There was a young fellow
from Tonga

Whose donger grew longer
and longer

So he had it away

In a rather strange way

With a short-sighted,
seven-foot conger.

A sturdy young fellow in Poole

Was blessed with a marvellous tool.

When fully extended

The bloody thing ended

A couple of miles north of Goole.

I MET A YOUNG GIRL FROM HAVANA,

WHO WAS KNOWN FOR HER
DOWN-TO-EARTH MANNER.

SHE SAID: `BEG YOUR PARDON,

BUT IS THAT A HARD ON,

AND IF NOT, WOULD YOU PASS
A BANANA?'

There was a young girl
from Dundrum,

Who swore she would never succumb,

But she did, in the end,

With a friend of a friend,

Who helped her to come
with his thumb.

Well, here we both are in the hay

And I'm dying to have a good lay,

For a red-blooded male

Likes a nice bit of tail

But this one has fur and says 'Neigh!'

The Campbells, the couple next door,

Are over-sexed people, I'm sure,

And it sounds by the shrieks

And the way their bed creaks

That the Campbells are coming once more.

A foolish old codger from Goring

Was asked why he'd taken up whoring.

'It's simple,' he said,

'My wife is stone dead,

And necrophilia's simply
dead boring.'

A HORNY YOUNG BUTCHER CALLED MARCUS

WAS FOUND IN THE FREEZER QUITE STARKERS,

HIS PRICK TURNING BLUE

WHILE ATTEMPTING TO SCREW

THE REAR OF A FRESHLY HUNG CARCASS.

Whenever I've nothing to do,

I jerk myself off – well, don't you?

In fact, I'm so slick

At jerking my dick

That I've no inclination
to screw!

I'M IN LOVE WITH A YOUNG FEMALE COPPER,

WHO LOVES TO BE SCREWED GOOD AND PROPER,

WHICH IS ALL VERY FINE,

BUT WE SCREW ALL THE TIME

AND I'VE BLISTERS ALL OVER MY CHOPPER.

I ONCE KNEW A FELLOW
CALLED SCOTTY,

WHOSE HABITS WERE
AWFULLY GROTTY:

IN FIVE MINUTES FLAT

HE HAD BUGGERED
MY CAT

AND TOSSED HIMSELF
OFF IN MY POTTY.

A dusky young maiden from Goa

Invited me upstairs to show her

A kinky position

For having coition,

Then gave me a tenner to blow her.

I wish I knew more about Jim's

Unusual sexual whims,

Many of which

Involve pneumatic tits

And synthetic, customised quims.

A sexually naive young sailor,
Concerned about being a failure,
Was screwed every day
In the nautical way
By the crew of a Japanese whaler.

When Martin screwed Maud on his pillion,

He said to her, 'Maud, thanks a million,

I love a tight twat

But yours beats the lot

And my penis is turning vermilion!'

A vulgar young fellow
called Janus

Could fart the 'Last Post'
through his anus.

He may think it's smart

And call it an art,

But I think young Janus
is heinous.

No wonder the French mistress hates

That randy young bugger called Bates.

He just has to catch

A whiff of her snatch

And young Master Bates masturbates.

A silly old farmer from Wendover

Told his busty young milkmaid
to bend over,

Then he planted his tool,

Till his wife said, 'You fool,

You're shoving it up the
wrong end of her.'

Though parting can be such a shame;

Their marriage has not been the same;

Since she found him sunk

To his bollocks in spunk

Up the arse of the pantomime dame.

I once knew a girl

called Annetta,

Who bought an enormous
red setter,

Which licked her left tit,

Then nuzzled her slit

Till she couldn't say stop.
Then it ate her.

When Angus was
kicked out of Troon

For farting too loud
out of tune,

The big ignoramus

Plugged up his anus

And now he's a
weather balloon.

I really don't think our
stenographers

Should pose in the nude
for photographers.

These shots of pudenda

Will only engender

The interest of back-street
pornographers.

There was a fine fellow
called Avery,

Whose spunk was
uncommonly savoury.

His missus, of course,

Found it cheaper than
sauce,

And it made all her stews
taste more flavoury.

Our teacher of maths is a Scot,

But tight she is certainly not.

In fact, we deduce,

That by regular use,

We have **doubled** the size
of her twat.

A rather gay actor called Fox

Was often found
down in the docks

In his favourite role,

Which was filling his hole

With big, burly
stevedores' cocks.

Look, Doctor,
I don't think it's funny

To be told,
when I've spent so much money,

That your diagnosis

Is **myxomatosis**

From having it off with a bunny!

 **WHEN THE GOOD LORD CREATED MY DINAH,**

HE DIDN'T TAKE CARE TO DESIGN HER

THE WAY THAT HE SHOULD HAVE

OR HE NEVER WOULD HAVE

LEFT SANDPAPER UP HER VAGINA.

Gipsy Rose Lee, wife of Sid,

Was famed for the

dances she did:

As everyone knows,

She wore very few clothes,

And she'd show you her

quim for a quid.

Said Malcolm McTavish
from Bute,

As he buggered a male
prostitute:

"Well, the love of my life

Has run off with my wife,

So one has to find some
substitute."

A lively young lass from Blantyre

Succumbed to her lover's desire

And, when he was in,

Jabbed his arse with a pin,

Which made him go in even higher.

That cunning old codger
called Custer

Would make the maid feel all
a-fluster,

For the lecherous flirt

Would lift up her skirt

And tickle her quim with a
duster.

Sue has spent so much time
in the sack,
Taking big hairy cocks
up her crack,
With macho young men
Coming time and again,
That she's slipped every disc
in her back.

Old Tom was the talk of
Nantucket,

If anything moved
he would fuck it:

He was up a girl guide

On the night that he died –

A fine way of kicking
the bucket!

A LUSTY YOUNG LASS
FROM TOLEDO

ENCOUNTERED A WAYWARD
TORPEDO.

WHICH SHE STARTED
TO SCREW

THEN IT WENT OFF
AND BLEW

A BLOODY GREAT HOLE
WHERE SHE PEED-O.

When Fred started
farting like thunder,

He got quite concerned,
and no wonder,

And he corked up his
ass

So the gas could not
pass

Then he blew his whole
backside asunder!

A FORTUNATE FELLOW CALLED SANDON

WAS BORN WITH A SEVEN-INCH
STAND ON.

THE MIDWIFE SAID, `GOD,

HOW EXCEEDINGLY ODD!´

AS HE SHAGGED HER
WITH CAREFREE ABANDON.

Tim took out his stiffy to stuff it

Up the welcoming cunt of
Miss Muffet

But, try as he might,

Her cunt was too tight,

So Tim only managed to
muff it.

I once knew a kinky young lass,

Who loved to shove things
up her ass:

If you studied her crap

You would find bits of scrap,

Such as ornaments made
out of brass.

Oh sexy, salacious
Miss Plum!

When I asked her which way
she had come,

She answered, 'By train.'

I replied, 'Come again?'

And she did, with my prick
up her bum.

A nasty old
fellow called Mark

Would wander
around after dark

Getting his kicks

Doing perverted tricks

With nude
statuettes in
the park.

We really must treat with more gravity

The numerous acts of depravity

Of those two nasty queers

Who've been at it for years

Called Ben Doone and Philip
McCavity.

Look, darling, I'm not blaming you

For this tampon I've found in the stew:

The taste is okay

But please take it away

It is not very easy to chew!

I'M IN LOVE WITH A FELLOW CALLED FRANK

WITH A COCK LIKE THE GUN ON A TANK,

AND THERE'S NOTHING SO GRAND

AS TO TAKE HIM IN HAND

AND GIVE HIM A JOLLY GOOD WANK.

When Jane wore her black leotard
My pecker grew horny and hard,
So we had it away
Without further delay
And there wasn't a single hole
barred.

A pretty young waitress called Glenda,

Was a flower of the feminine gender,

Till one day, by mistake,

She made cherry milkshake

By catching her tits in the blender.

Of lovers I've had
quite a few

But none of them thrilled me
like you,

Your fabulous twat

Is so juicy and hot

That it drives me quite wild
when we screw.

SO LET'S RAISE OUR GLASSES
TO PAT,

WHO HAS MANAGED, IN TEN
MINUTES FLAT,

TO SUCK OFF THE SEMEN

OF FIVE ABLE SEAMEN,

THE MATE AND THE
ADMIRAL'S CAT.

A nasty young man from Japan

Attempted to rape Marianne,

But the end of his gender

Snapped her suspender

Which shot off his balls with a twang.

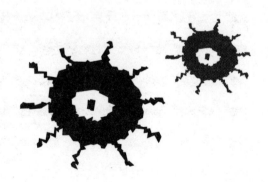

A shepherd, who had a prize flock,

Believed it might improve the stock

If he rogered each one,

So he started at dawn,

But by noon he had ruptured his cock.

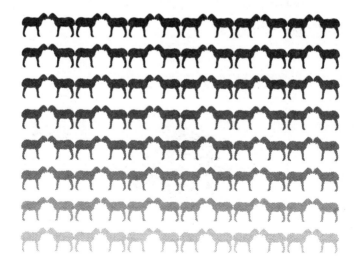

I'm finding it
incomprehensible,

That an otherwise
seemingly sensible

And serious chap

Could write all this crap

It really is quite
reprehensible!